NO HARM DONE

laurance wieder/ NO HARM DONE

ardis/ann arbor

Copyright©1975 by Ardis, 2901 Heatherway Ann Arbor Mich 48104.
ISBN 0-88233-086-1 (cloth), 0-88233-087-X (paper). Laurance Wieder,
NO HARM DONE.

CONTENTS

A March Afternoon [11]

A Bottomless Scheme [13]

The Bare Resolve [14]

No Harm Done [17]

Hastening Thus [18]

Guide to the Perplexed [22]

Heartsease [25]

Apostrophe [27]

A Golden Measure [29]

So High, So Low [31]

Crusade Song [33]

These Things Do Not Happen [35]

A Letter to his Sister [38]

Opening a Snapdragon [39]

With the Voice [42]

Jingle [43]

Invocation [45]

The Poetry Reading: A Masque [56]

NO HARM DONE

A MARCH AFTERNOON

People keep telling me I'm too abstract,
Abstruse, obscure, disjunct, they can't
Get what I'm driving at, but really
It's very easy to understand:
I hear voices
And description bores me
So I write what I hear
And let you see what you want.

Actually, just being direct and simple
Is harder than it looks:
It needs the force that powers heroes on despite
Dust heaped on the head, the thorny bed, the images the bad ones made
Them feel was the true picture.
Writing out of rural retirement,
That whole business of what's out there
Undermines the vastness of my productions,—
After all, it's just what you think,—
And leaves uneasy residuals when
What's called for is the recognition
That the body sleeping near me's a near stranger
And it's your spirit, dearest, that's familiar,
A forbidden city.
The pilgrimage makes a holy one
Of even modest me, who tended to ignore
What the guide remarked as detail
And while we were walking, chose
To think of the almost real rowboat
Really floating, away from the moorings,
Where the hours parked.

I experienced the uneasy cloudiness that it all
Had been before of old etcetera
But, when I stopped to analyze my eerie feelings
I found them insubstantial

11

And the red hills neither grew nor shrank
Below the gray sky, but gables and widow walks
Did look a little different, as though
Painted from an earlier master's work.

A BOTTOMLESS SCHEME

Ours is a less opulent doom, born
Into bad times which won't get better
Or the best times which still
Not what they were began receding
As we saw them in the first light of the afternoon
The cold snow dancing down like molecules upon the air
And voices behind windows
And no constancy

THE BARE RESOLVE

The only thing to do's become the life of those impassable times
Which fear or love excuses, a short and unrecoverable term
Set down beside this waywardness an everduring theme, the transit
Of all navigations beneath the sun, which doesn't let up
For a moment, which constant presence makes of us
The children we once were within the cowl of songs
That swim leviathan upon the inward stream: ah, love
(The lamest claim of all) makes it all right, the lucid folly
Bodies swim toward, the streamy sense
That flows through slices of what life calls life.

New Year's this year broke warm and clear. The neighbors
Marched their families from house to house: the timelessness
Of those revisitations promise lives won't be deranged,
Not even in the leafless shadows January throws back to the trees
Where they again debark along the causeway, warned couples
Who see into each other what their hopes point toward:
The truth of love at seventeen eternal, devoted children
Grown past twenty. Where are the pictures past we hoped to age towards?
What is our true position? The bare walls take the picture
With alacrity. Light is the substance of complaint.

In autumn bees dance for their rueful sakes. The winter sparrows
Spring their summered songs. Age freshens up those first impressions
Which wax wild or woeful in the windows of a weird one
Never would have guessed at, never for a moment, how the hags
Pronounced the old clichés with relish, knowing we would take to them
Eventually, not counting on the cheer that rings
Around and through the records of our time and makes a music
Of the dolors pioneers lament for: do voices'
Banners flap above the heads of armies, or do they flock
To the standard, pied and grateful for some sense of sense?

There is a note the violin was made to play, a destination
That each car's been built for. One trusts not in the picture

14

Of usefulness, but in the justice of the final arrangement, no matter
How obscure. And that exalts us, lets us godlike see
No gods but powers nonetheless upon the stream by which
All moves, on which the poet muses in the words that bring
This mastery to light (from light it comes), and which returns
The bride to her first bed, which radiance
Darkness alone outnumbers, and that's the clamorous point
Our toil turns on.

What we remember is all that keeps, all that's remembered
Is long life, or words, or wisdom, but
For balance in the face of passage, hands
Open, water runs, drink lips can touch and holding
The breeze close at bedtime, draw their daughters
To us, saying whatever must be said
Before the ghost ships surging from the sea
Arrive with pipes and castanets to take us
To the new.world, far from here, from bells
And bulbs and chairs and rugs and desks in small apartments.

There is plenty of time now to consider all that stumped me, now
That it's decided that what purified me was not suffering
Reluctantly relinquished, but barely living
Through the days like water acquiescing,—time later for the grandeur
Of the given world, and rather like the sun on a dull day
The light that is our poetry refloods the provinces
That afternoon and morning divvied up between them, all the living
Singing chanteys underneath the stars with names
To steer by. My sympathies, not out there
In the landscape, nonetheless take the picture for their own:

Perhaps not the resolve at all, but the acceleration
Of these times has caused the trappings of what's stable
To exeunt the orbit, omnes, flotsam, jetsam, tailings
In the wake of the as yet unmeasured progress which intends
To make the port the sirens sing of.
I'm not sure I've checked my northern drift.
It may be that some larger force has carried me this far
And will go further than I might have guessed, but what returns

15

Me to myself is like reunion with old places, a one-sided affair
Between the somber truth and this clear winter day.

Are we reeds that we dry up and whistle, rattle in the windy bog,
Have hopes or feel resentful of our fellows? To be grand and sweet and
Resonant and generous is not writ on the cards that shuffle past,
Nor are the harmonies we have laid hold of. At best
A gawky version of a marble idol, at worst cold and rooted
Like the original lump, without debauching the deathless consistency
Our fathers left us, one comes to terms with that shameful body
Where the image dwelt and shuffles with the coils love and labor,
Vine divine, ardor in the arbor, winds the sheets before
A breeze that's always freshening.

NO HARM DONE

The last day of July: the sun is out
And time seems many papers folded over,—
Out, in the way a light goes out,
Relentless. But that imputes some sense to light

And time seems many papers folded over.
Perhaps some useful fact will come to light, something
Relentless. But that imputes some sense to light
Which has no sense, and has nothing to indicate.

Perhaps some useful fact will come to light, something
Navigable by the backward sense
Which has no sense, and has nothing to indicate
But, as a great sphere, meets my feet,

Navigable by the backward sense,
Across the smoky lawns and sidewalks of twenty years ago.
But, as a great sphere meets my feet,
The trek is effortless and irresistible.

Across the smoky lawns and sidewalks of twenty years ago,
The last day of July. The sun is out,
(The trek is effortless and irresistible)
Out in the way a light goes out.

HASTENING THUS

When I was ten my family went to Europe,
Not with an organized tour group,

But in a Fiat. In Paris, however, we
Took a bus tour, which I remember distinctly:

Our first stop was the Montmartre
And Le Sacre Coeur (one place combining God and art

As was explained in four languages): the white
Cathedral rode a cloud above the mount, in the light

Of that August afternoon. Knowing nothing of absinthe,
I wasn't interested then in tales of bohemian poets and painters who
                lived a marginal but rich existence in those narrow streets
                at the turn of the last century, although I might be since.

We stopped next at Notre Dame in the Ile de France.
(Until then I thought the Ile was just a boat.) By chance

A Latin service was in progress,
So after taking in the lost art of stained glass,

I left the church interior
And went back to the square,

Which brings me
To the focus of my memory.

Carved figures of the Saints occupy a cleft
In the church facade. Halfway up, to the left

Stands a carving of St. Denis, his head under his arm,—
This caused my younger sister some alarm.

An analogy with decapitated chickens was rejected
By us both, as well as several less compelling explanations. Unperfected

Visions of the crucifixion haunted my sleep in Italy,
Along with other Catholic imagery,

But, among the urban scenery,
St. Denis' head remains most prominent in my memory.

There also was a Europe without parents:
Riding horseback in Villeneuve, swimming at Clarens,

Riding the funicular between Montreux and Glion
To camp, which overlooked the Chateau de Chillon.

In the castle dungeon I saw the pillar
Where Byron carved his name (I thought he was the prisoner),

And hikes above Glion, the rushing river and the rock
(Rochers des Nayes) where, on a small village green, a clock

Face planted with summer blooms.
There is a corner in the rooms

Of memory, even when the sun stays, dark
And dreadful. There, where two walls intersect the floor, a spark

Curves on the joint of three dimensions. Fear
And chaos, monsters from the id, all the crude mater-

Ials of life live there, and it was also in late August, on a hike
In the Dents du Midi near the French border, that I saw night

Crash into those red cliffs, and saw (quite literally) the way
That space yawns. That day

We campers went out for a walk on a path
Threading the edge of a 3,000-foot cliff. Half

19

Of us marched single file toward a bluff that overlooked the "Tal."
The other half had turned back to make dinner. While

The sun dropped behind me I wished that I had brought
My camera, thinking "These mountains are as they are now once, and
                                                                      sought

For later never will appear as now." But
I had left my camera at the lodge. Thinking like that,

One camper broke into a run, he ran
Downhill along the edge before us calling "Look, look" and then

I knew that he would slip.
He hit a wet strip

On the path and toppled forward.
                    The mountains swim before a word

Can capture them, and that one shriek
I made then also rises from the corner, high and weak.

Later, back at the lodge, a counselor lost
His watch, which he decided had been stolen. Most

Of the night we sat on wooden benches in the summer chill
Waiting for the thief to confess. No one did. Until

The watch was found next to the Turkish toilet, we stayed
Awake. Since that day I have never played

Too close to the edge
Of any ledge,

Either a New York City
Roof, or rural gorge. I can be, and have been, witty

About annihilation, although it scares me.
And my memory, while it halts, never impairs me

20

While hastening thus,
Minus or plus.

GUIDE TO THE PERPLEXED

1

Chaos is a green line that surrounds the earth:
Both this world and vision hang by threads, and
If not the threads, the world or vision can get tangled

Though if only one of two is fouled, then a guide
Can pull the sense clear, which unravels as a spool
Of thread unravels, rolls away, so that a straight connection

Straightaway becomes more distant when the hand untangles,
Sorting out the silken from the flax, though heaven
Is a blue thread that sews up the earth, the power

Yoked in mass, and stitches the horizon
Fast to earth where red threads wind
Down to the water, the cast mirror of the sky,

Wet remnant of a clear, all-seeing eye
(The sun a pupil? What is dark) perplexes
And whose guiding power,

Likened to a hand,
Does not directly take in hand, but points,
A finger stirring dust in water.

2

The star that, almost risen
        Fell out of the sky,
And leaves would, if they fell

        Upwards, glue themselves
Discreetly to the oak:

In a world where nothing is forbidden
The joggers leap in tandem
    By the shadow of the lake.

What was the argument?
That there was such a thing as choice,
    A project launched toward rest:

The swift geese clatter by the moon
    Which happens to be full again.

Mushrooms know a colorless grief:
    The fatherless self
That was an odd one.

                    3

The lizards of the past grow into dragons.
Children are only innocent
When not compared to angels.

Beside the grave, all words turn into mirrors,
Reflecting what is left without the errors.
The lizards of the past grow into dragons.

When they get old, men
Dress up like sages and take off for the mountain.
When not compared to angels,

They glow and look substantial, since they walk
Before their children. While they talk,
The lizards of the past grow into dragons

Smitten by the heroes of emotion
And the "very life" itself seems a profession,
When not compared to angels.

Compared to old men, children all are demons:

                    23

They hum the pitch of morning into tangles.
The lizards of the past grow into dragons,
When not compared to angels.

HEARTSEASE

To the cat fancier, every cat is special.
    For the lover of trees, every leaf has its sway.
Lovers, in general, are particular, Cheryl,
    But that poses problems. To go the way
Of little voices
    Makes difficult choices
Harder still. The clouds' shape dissolves
    And gives the clouds shape.
Nothing can hold them. Not bars or the earth.
    I remember waking up early one morning
In my dorm room in Switzerland:
    Early gray, the day so new
And quiet I had no voice
    So I lay still, looking out the window.
Clouds flew past, shaped like reindeer,
    Mickey, Donald, docile horses of the sky
And no one saw them—only I
    Remember those formations
Which I'll never see again
    If indeed I saw them then.
White paddle steamers cross the water
    Between Geneva, Vevey and Lausanne.
To ride on one
    Was not so much fun
As watching them while walking
    Home after swimming
In the lake wind below the peaks
    And hearing the boats bell
And splash. I felt hollow
    Like a reed, but deeper
And I wanted to hold it all if I could,
    To take the living picture kept
Alive. For others.
    The light of afternoon will pass
Through glass to glass, time's fountain

25

Foot glides through the sky, while
The first man, in his splendor, didn't last.
        I may be poor, but I am not confused.
I may be getting old, but I understand
        Age doesn't take away, it adds
Clouds to clouds, pillow on pillow, day
        To day until they grow solid, and I see more
Now than when I was younger
        And nothing was new. See, we are short,
But the fires run cold above us
        Who are sliding
In and out of the gray sky. Contending
        With the women in my life, I turned
Once to the clouds, once to the healed water that the boats
        Wake, and once again to comfort
In the work. No great conclusion, while the muscles
        Carry us to different heights, more
Measurable, as though we ever knew them.

APOSTROPHE

The nameless
Dread that once was thought the essence
Of the mystery
I can't remember, the sense
That what looks passing now
Is passing: souls
Sound quiet after sunset,
Trace some source
Of heat or light to read by,
Beat against the panes that parcel
Time and place where trees applaud
The bridges that erected stand
Truthfully, for what men don't know
Irks them, and gloom-bird like, equates
Their fears and things half known
With the circumference of the sun, the truth's
Feet facing us, a picture
Of both peril and the charms
All lives by, ditties
To the rock and creek, sports with
Amaryllis, shades
Cold wafers of content, so blue
And casual enclosure, sky
A page for alphabetic herons,
Slate that writes the tone
Of switches, you we whistle through
And under you we carry both
The pressure that carries and the one
That carries off.

So here must be the better place,
This plain where puddles prick them past
And married first
To local fates, we unlike
The departed wonder why

27

The key glints in the sun, entranced
That this might be the entrance to hereafter
We stand below what rises, listening
To voices' fathers tell it all
Again, those times
They wake for, and beliefs
March with icicles across roped eaves, with
Winter constellations in a summer sky.

A GOLDEN MEASURE

As I've gotten older, I've realized
Or rather felt that I am only here
On sufferance: maybe it's because I haven't sat
At my own table, or slept in my own bed for over a year
But I continue for the sake of what clamors
Inside me, the charge I carry
Carries me off in fits, it fits
I suppose, into some scheme, and the power that suffers me
May not be
Visible, but it is felt as surely as a silk hand
Feels the velvet wind around

I have accepted your invitation to the dinner
Of human wisdom, read the sacred texts and all the comments
on them,
Have taken my companion for a life into my life
And marched on the trusting center of the mystery
Which, after all the years that pass have passed,
Will be revealed, and probably small,
How I should have known it all along
And you, who also grieve for what's dropped out
Holes in memory, who remember the voice but, after a few weeks, forget
The touch, who find such closeness impossible in thought,
You will feel better too, will feel the good
That visits in a human touch. We have become mortal
So we might live and learn
Just what the world is all about, we loom
The life, we weave (the husband and the wife)
Short threads on the endless fabric, knitted
To the dark sail of night, and loft the lighter linen
Of a day. Hot, the snow lifts off the lawn,
The ways of men reopen in the thaw, while the consistency
Of coming and going imparts that inconsistent freak,—
Meteors in our sky,—and only to the gods
It's never random. I am given

29

The lucid gift for hours at a time
And by that light will lead us both
Through the mirror, through the wall
To a place where the earth shakes
Only rarely, where lakes look like cups
Of sky, and the red hills change back to the color
That they were before they changed to what they are
Now, smoother, levelled by the windy allegory of the elements

The royal road is unrepeatable, we never
Twice descend, and so don't fear
The past, the shoelace of the common place is all
That happens over, and those mists you felt
Rising in the Fens of When are only breath
And warmth that fogs our window on eternity

SO HIGH, SO LOW

"I am remember the time, in Italy
Where Girolamo took my friend aside
(He couldn't say this to my face) he said
'Jimmy, he used to be a good radical
But America spoil him, he is not
Like me.' What the hell. Forty,
Fifty years ago we all think, all
But me, 'The Communist,' but
Kropotkin, he say then, and I agree
That if the Communist keep going
(This was 1921) the way they go
In twenty year the world will come
To hate the name of Russia.

But maybe I have changed, and maybe
None of us be what we think we are:
We want the money, we take it easy,
We get fat and grow the hair.
The children don't think how we do,
They don't want the dollar, but
They call themselves the radical. Pfui.
They call names at the police.
In Italy the priest and the policeman
Would kill you, and nobody waste his time
With names. One time when I work
On the ships (I just come to America)
I meet a friend, a anarchist, and he
Want me to run the whiskey with him
Because we fight together against
The Communist. 'You must be crazy,'
I said. 'You do this and you only find the trouble,
And what is your life then?'

                    Henrietta, now
She's stopped the work, we both

31

Have time to go to opera. We watch
The television on the Watergate, but any country
That give you only two choice for the election
What can you expect? No difference
Between the one man and the other.
All of them make the people to hate
The name of government. Only the anarchist
Is any good. Only the anarchist, and I
Say this after more than seventy years living
And I always say this, like the Prince
Kropotkin say in 1921."

CRUSADE SONG

These feats of earth shall bring us to the air.
The past caught fright like colds
And old guitars hymn our libidos
Which guide us with Orlando and his birdbrain
Legions on to Bethlehem. The broad plain falls
Away from the Glum Mountains. Are we Turks
Or Huns or Tatars that we hang before the sack
With camels passing? Equals must remain
The same, even in the green and mortal eye
Our company berates the old administration
Who draw their bathrobes off beside the Jordan.

Leave us not grow torpid peccaries back home.
Our death is not so dear as what we know.
Nothing has been done anyway, for troubadors
To sing into a lady's hearth.
Remember history! Remember Scipio Africanus
And Alexander! Save your rice for bread
And can the marriage rites! There is a gauze
That overlies what shall be done, and your grandsons
Will look back to now with pleasure, thinking
Then, then men were men, there was revenge,
Adventure, and no foes besmirched the almanacs.

God leases out his salve. Our wounds will heal
With our hiccups, and the fright will pass
And we will rest, andirons, each with his fellow
And the fond boats will lie along the pillars
Rising and falling in the fans that turn the tides.
We shall be martyrs to the winds, the very winds that nightly
Crown the pines and meadows of our dear Provence.
At that fair house no churl dare to complain,
And the shepherd calls the Caliph's grandson, his retainer
To carry out the slops, or fan the forge
Which heats the blade that made the Moslem melancholy.

33

Our song sounds like the edges of the neap tide,
Our companions dressed like falcons poised to swoop,
Our marks the iron mountain and the lion,
We come like flames from Flanders to the flat grainfields here
And fire our French-forged lances at the spaces
Turk dogs dare to fill. Grr. A red and sober hour.
They'll wish they'd slept with cobras in their camp
Or straggled at the Bosporus and drowned
Rather than face the terrors of our conquest,
A face more terrible than twenty sieges without water in the Sudan
And the troops of Caesar lurking at the gate.

Draw a pot for the collector of uproar.
Beware, o snake, beware the mailed heel.
Death, do not think to eat our company,—
It's not your fate: we're all going
To Paradise, in style, like Elijah.
The passive mares of passage clear our way.

French horses, raised within the moated fastness
Nose their enemies aside with evening oats
And grazing as they go, 'til not one blade remains
Below the heavy bells around their necks
And death shall no more visit them, than shall the phoenix
Fly into the sun again, with all our company.

THESE THINGS DO NOT HAPPEN

1

Unlike the king who chained four eagles to his throne
And, tempting them with meat, thought to reach heaven
I can't force the birds to eat my words, and where
We lined up for the comedy, the picnic was consumed.

2

It's unlikely
That the change will overtake us here
Between the trellis and the outdoor barbecue.
Peter, Nina, Richard, Mark and Jimmy
Sitting with friends of a lifetime.
O native country, royal realm of Troy!
O gods' house, Ilion, full of joy!

3

Today I thought about you, how
When you are older and the world comes to no point
You may look back on our horseback conversations
And see two people riding in a ring. The dust
Won't make it to the sun. Our words, however,
Can be heard above the expressway,—
A teenage girl who left the flute for horses,
Who plans to ride for years without a break.

4

Eddie pushes a wheelbarrow full of haybales through the stable yard
Late in the afternoon, a single rider
Canters through the maple trees.
Golf courses have eaten up the local fields, the players
Vocal, clubs hiss at the tees.

35

5

"I like that, 'Heaven
Is the earth run smoothly.' I remember waking up
On an August night like this, and you would whistle
'Meadowlands' at Paul's window.
It's the machines that weaken us.
The air conditioning goes into my head.
But we went to Jerusalem, and saw
The Austro-Hungarian post office
Steps where Josi's grandfather would watch the mail boat
Sail in with letters from Budapest. Every stone
There has a name, and every place
A meaning. We washed our feet
With three old Moslem women (it was Friday)
And with them stood next to Jacob's well."

6

You are going to be happy for the rest of your life.
Nothing will be withheld from you
Now that you have learned not to ask
The living will be drawn toward you
The way an ivory handle attracts slips of paper
When it's rubbed against a sweater.

That's very nice, but what about the evil in the world?
Tao says there are three evils. First
The one you can change with your hand (the smallest);
Next, the one changed with the pen (that's larger); then
The one you can change only in your heart.

"The Tao," said the old doctor, "was a very great sage."

And so we remembered Plato's Shining Example:

7

Taking the heat's ease beneath the green cathedral trees
While kids chase balls, flee from the bees
The old horizon holds us, hand in hand, in time

That gathers up the facts
And puts them on the table, or the human sea
Washes down the streets where life gets older, more
Mysterious, and one by one we learn to let it go:
The kites, the silver snakes swim through the breeze
Where sirens rise and fall, aloof
From that intelligence, despotic, that announces
I am nearly free, and finishes
Again the ancient world.

A LETTER TO HIS SISTER

It was hard for you to put up with your older brother
Who doesn't ask properly for permission to arrive,
Who arrives under his own clouds, and who sleeps,
Almost sick, in the living room just when the sun
Is best, in afternoon. You are right to bridle
At my intrusion. But I wonder what you're doing.
The new puppy has a sweet disposition, but you
Make no attempt to housebreak her, and I am afraid
She will settle into bad habits. Don't you see
The kitchen shouldn't be a kennel? You tell yourself
"Not now. I will be gone for weeks, and when I come back
Then she will be trained." Meanwhile, a bad smell
Lingers in the kitchen, and time is passing.
I wonder if you see your own ideas, as I see
I am awkward. I don't want you to get angry with me,
But feel you would be mistaken to put off training
Your young dog, who grows faster than you or I,
And soon must be something more than sweet.

OPENING A SNAPDRAGON

1

The sky is cloudy, cloudy soul.
    A bee wings through the clouded bowl.
The wind blows out a chilly glass.

    Days turn to us. Our eyes are open.
Hear the creepers growing down.
    Growing made me feel finer.

Drawn through water running faster.
    Sleeping on a sleeping tiger.

    I think there is a world to come.
Much like this one, only better.

    It's October, trees are balding
From the top down. Yet to find
    A day when nothing happens.

2

A day when nothing happens
    When the dry sun walks abroad
And brings out the gray ladies

    Those who suffer from the cold
Who call down curses on the human beings
    And ask to be brought back as hippos

Wading wild in Africa, as cannibals
    In this, the world that was
Or dark earth raising up and tearing down

39

As brittle ice, as flinders flown
As glass glints on the dun sand
The neighbors leap from the low sycamore

Onto the lower leaves. Pitiful
Because they are so many, like the sages
Riding out on foamy visions

"This is it" and "This is it"
Join to all the great discoveries, radiant
And uncompromising, like their chains

3

Radiant and uncompromising, like their chains
My mother held a snapdragon
Between her thumb and index finger

She squeezed the base of the flower
Opening the dragon's mouth, and barked, and said
This is why it's called a snapdragon.

Mums and zinnias grew there too
And the climbing rose afflicted
With Japanese beetles. Pachysandra packed

The sandy bed below the chokecherry.
Hollyhock, philodendron, rhodedendron and hydrangea
Bloomed in front of the garage.

And I would climb out the upstairs dormer window
To understand how the roof slanted
Without falling off the roof. Today

A clear one. The mysteries keep
To themselves, like the bottom of the river.
You are just the same as ever.

4

You are just the same as ever, living
 On the paper in our world, our world in the session of mists.
Aloof, aloft, awash, or leaning toward the sea

 Wanting only to be good, loved, remembered
Like a lake, a slice of toast is also sweet and part
 Of something smaller, the abuses of the past.

I'm calling you, you wrists that fleck the foam, because
 I like to hear your name, that sounds
Like rocks below the sea of Maine. I see them

 When I can, on this occasion, swept
By herons in a line across the water, breaking
 With the orange sun behind.

WITH THE VOICE

Today was luminous, a wonder.
The snow came with a clap
And fell like platters
From the 10th of April sky.

I consider it a sign that winter's over.
Or rather, it's as much a sign as anything
Full of light and angles:

Echoes with the voice
Of a man walking out, of water
On the dogwood bark.

JINGLE

I've written poems on benches,
On the beach, in trains, in cars, on planes
Winging west and south, in bed
But mostly sitting at my desk, sober,
Drunk and walking up Broadway, drunk
And sitting on a stoop, sick, recovering,
In dire straits, in ecstasy, in stern moods,
Calm and panic, out of vanity, from hatred
Of my vanity, for vengeance, as rebuke,
Reply, riposte, return, thrust, stroke,
Caress and missile of an upset, poems
Of good and evil and the stuff that falls
Between them, falls like leaves
Or starlight from out there, sinking
To my knees or rising
To the drama of a small occasion, with wit
Or lackwit luster, clusters of love
Poems, wise poems, prose poems,
Poems of far ports and poems from homes,
    Rhymes and forms,
    Tunes in storms
    To cool madness
    To expel sadness
    Like held breath
    To do away with death
    (Not possible) in life—
    Poems won me a sharp wife,
    A badly paid position,
    A view of the dust that clouds
    A view of the dust that clouds,
    A portable typewriter, ten cartons of books,
    The esteem of the powerless,
    The love of the married,
    The praise of professors,
    Discounts from doctors,

A place with the gods
That no one believes in,
Some music on records,
A view of the sidewalk
From a wrought-iron balcony
Through French doors, high and airy
And a feeling the future
Will wake up and hug me
Like March air when the wind dies
And flowers fall open

INVOCATION

I

This edge
Must be where the present lies, descended
From the sky's harmonious loans
Faced by the panes of sleep: murmuring walls
Divide us and the very moment from
Eternity, or perhaps now
Is oblivion and this the ladder
To an eminence of trees, applause, for the unanimous earth
Recedes, I sing in limbs winds hurdle
Leaves in the brown shadow of a vortex.

Having charged myself this way, the sparks
Then sought a screen where they
Could dance their naked dance without
Being molested, so they cast a net, and then
O wing and voice
                    divulge the flight of eagles
Traces where the clouds depend
Fast by that mountain voices drive the rain down
And I am no longer
Nestled in the eaves, I am
That bark whose sail sets the winds that fix and change.

The trees and wet grass disappeared
When I looked out the window after lunch
I watched the snow swirl and rise
Like devilled dust,—the gray sun panted
Through its blinds and tolling panels as I whispered
This must be the wilderness:
The flat and shadow of that mountain pulse
The way all voices are consumed, and there
Before me, one
Who floated to us in the reeds.

45

His eyes were brighter then
Than they had ever been before
And his clear words lured water
From the rocks and dust and charmed
(So we thought) breakfast from the clouds.
Aged, fed by promises and honey, he led
Our walk a long time. In one hand
He clutched the start of time,—the other held
As in the knot that bridles anger
Law, as he knew men
Must be compelled where they are not forbidden
And that fruit,
Ripened, fills

Its own descending shadow in the hollow sand.
The sun directly overhead, we trudged
Foreshortened by the sharp rays nearly blinded towards
A garden only he could see
And not with our help, how
Reaching that river once again
The water heaped beside our children.
As the wake closed, currents
Carry off our footprints so
That only words remain of all this living.

The law
Breaks weighed
Against these wants: cliffs yield to the wind
Eventually, and vacuums and vapors, longer
And so more relentless outlast men
Who, insatiable, briefly resemble
Death's image, casting nets
Into the water, we are taken
Gasping, fish, surprised.
But he was prepared, that day
That he was born he crept away.

Who can watch his father
Knows the space he left

46

(Bed slightly warm, depression in the atmosphere)
Knows grief as the suspension
Linking days of work to days of work
Never suspended, still
The sons of men cross gorges on such overpasses
Shouting "Grandfather" to steam that drifts up from below
And, still born, men come in
With festivals and clamor, claiming
Now to be the summit of creation.

II

The sun rose again today.
Is there no rest?
This is my time on earth, this
My place wherever I appear and move
Toward where I disappear and with me
All these people, jars with voices, time:
Is it the wind or wall that leans against the wind
That drives us into blizzards, or the drift
Accumulated, or am I the wind, the wall, the drift
The storm itself, and does rage pile
Spaces vowels leave in words to where

What evidence the pillars shed just lengthens
In the blue light of these afternoon inscriptions?
Only plain rock serves
To live on,—the shaping arts tend
To reduce such flocks as memory grazes
Back to the appearance of raw elements:
If that temple crumbles
Into the outline of itself,
Then reduction must be a principle
Of sound construction, and
Left out, space
Suggests intention, acorns
Light,
          the benches, beside rope

Dependent icicles, ramparts glare by
Sheets, the loom's thread, rather
Suggests an activity, the efflorescence
Of accident. But different.
                              Those alter-
Egos, spaces, space and object, choice,—the props
And index of impending order.

Who am I
To talk this way?
A rowboat drifts at random, sheltered
By the bay's arced shoal, constrained.
At sea the souls of dolphins drink the light
Which chains all space, light
Breaks the finned back breaking from the depths the
                              surface broke in, light
(O sole transmitted impulse of my distant source)
Mocks lakes, it falls, rises, beats, these oceans
Beat upon my shores.

                    A man composes
Chance on cubes and cards, sets the die
Or deck before whatever rolls the combers on the beach.
What is a cheat?
That pity
Might have force, wishes' fingers
Form the jetties of the soul, walls that neither wail
Nor make the ocean seem to yield
To a gesture.
                    Whose hand lifts me
From this eddy choked with reeds? What touch,
What question cradles me?
                              I should
Have not been born, or having been
I should have beat my shadow to the ground.
Here is no mystery, all plain as coming forward
Joining first the old men past, and then the earth itself
A cup, these oceanic feelings, drunk, as living things
The earth is thirsty,—solid men sink down

48

With seeds that splash at random on the yellow dirt.

A bird's wing soaring forward on the squall line out to sea.
The wing is fixed, is fast, it takes
The breath of flight for thunder.
O! to be an augur and bore a hole in the flat sky
So I might hear the sentence that my birdflight traces but
I never left the earth.

What woe I hear there, howling
Pricked by roses and the snow's
Thorns, hovers at the windows.
Pointed, day must pierce the pile of what came before.
What the light just touches, shows
And is no more.
The toppled beds of winter, words resist like flowers
Heliotropic bend aligned by speckled hours
Dense, attuned to the intensity
Trees emanate their children, violently
With all that's vertical
And green leaves fill brown spaces children trample.

The cry has past. The smoke
Which swallows stacks small birds against the wind.
Thin whistles rise upon the finger of our chances, pointing
To the east, the home
Of sunlight fills up local puddles, silver rope unloosened, and
                                                              the knot
Which ten times bellowed "let" into the void before I ever
                              tumbled into light now ten times whispers
"No" and bodies warp like swans
Who dunk their heads below the surface of the standing pool,
Waves generated billow breaking mirrored willows

And the world breaks
Into what falls away and what is left
Of which the swan's arched neck is an apostrophe
And whose return, o holy one, I greet
Perpetually what you have begun.

49

III

Who looks for the force that drives the rain down
Rises, but with
What words do I greet whatever follows?
How to call men to honor that they cannot see
Without, which lets
Men choose to baffle wind chimes after sunset or
To clench the light in one fist and the weight their words bear in another,
The moving image of a vapor, which transparent, waves like snakes
                                                    prophetic
Changed into what we must reduce to at the last,
Sound and light, how
To praise you at the morning meal, to think
That what appears could not outnumber what is hidden as the dead
Sleep in the shadows of a multitude of memories and names, while you
Who are the light, have none, no name
That thanks may take.

Is the sky a mirror of the earth as water is
An image of the sky?
                    And ships, tents pitched before the wind.

These frictions generate some light, as surfaces
Emerge because the dust or rime must settle there.
Things are not things, they are
What's noticed, marks of life,
Of chance but also fathered by intention.
Made known, no act is casual: no motion does not bear
The laws of motion out, and as the body feels
Right or wrong, all that shape includes and shade
Align along the edge where nothing stayed but left
Its traces on me.
                    I once sat

50

At that inclusive height, receiving strict instructions.
Below, men carried messages of lightning for the thunder.
Which doesn't mean that I must be somebody, but
Grown learned, that I stand
Both on the point and in the interval between the beaches and
$\qquad$ the driven sea.

Remarks in passing also bear
Whatever pinions carry words aloft, or stake
The burden of a wager to the earth:
Where I began could only lead me here for good
Or evil, as the light itself divides.
Nothing seeks to snare a man, face averted by the wind, infused
By all the distance covered
That one circle I described to call the rain down
Has erased such traces of what came before
As can be, so all might briefly
Flower in season, lots, and poetry
Also flourish as a picture of our passage.

Because I cannot help but choose,
Because I have been brushed by random fingers,
Because whatever happens backwards flows towards its mountain
$\qquad$ source by forking
As the scattering of rivers,
Because no word casts a shadow or can waste the wind
I choose what I say carefully
As care is all that can be taken in that wind
That weaves and bears the world away.

A man must offer to the incensed sky
His children, words that they know not,
Exotic words that are the gods our fathers knew not,—
Division's children snare the strands of that one rope
Whose blue coils bind the sea, whose tail
Twitches, the clear day recoils, and clarity
Emerges as the veil of emergency, the crest
At last crashing across the shoal, the bark
Borne smoothly sails into port.

51

Some things go unexpressed, building up intolerable pressure.
Uninterpreted, portents loom, statues bleed, owls shriek in disembodied
places voices jar, eclipses, migrations:
The passage jagged, revolutionary.
Transfixed by shapes that shatter and reform on the sea's face,
Stirring faces in the water, humming bits of melody, a man
Thinks the whole world hears him—hummers, crankers, barks and
passengers they pilot
Follow not even a sinking star, but meteors that freak
Night's jet petals and then tail off into the quick obscure impalpable
abyss reserved for those betrayed in hopes
Pity calls tragic: words
The best and worst of men, bless and buoy, bring to light.
Or, grown light themselves, they cast no shadow on the surface of the sea
And none who tend the weighty letters then can spell what wind
Wrote on the surface or what figures swim below there
At what depth.

IV

Words first appeared at sunset, so that night would never be completely
dark
And men could study, traveling through trackless spaces time describes
To that island where the dead talk to the living. On the beach beside the
sacrificial pool, they join
Who never touched, together in a world of thought
Which doesn't scatter as the rain, sweet water, scatters in the salt sea
Or the voices of aspirant trees
Rooted both in the dense earth, drinking that, and pointing toward
the sky:
The leaves, their children, the wind bears away, or is it just that place a
name marks out, our souls, that flip
and spiral
As the leaves do, rise in funnels
Through which words decant,—that cloud
Precedes all that a man can ever do, the mark that earth and air share him
Who wanders in the landscape of a vast intention chalked by what is
wanted and main chance, which adds
Streaks of its own, the master touch, that makes the canvas
Lifelike, arbitrary, leaves small wishes, war with what assails.

52

Trees, rooted, die where they are born, but we
Launch sable barks at an auspicious sunset, breeze freshening
And sail towards the seas' chains, to the utter mouth
Of a river so long that men living by its source have never dreamed such
                              a body as the sea might be forgotten
So their veins become the river piled by their bones in shadows on the
                              far side of the mountain:
At that mouth, by the new moon, the dead review
The world that they no longer have a share in.

Voices wash my beach as surf light heaved from the unsettled sea.

Unless they do inhabit trees,
Cry when twigs snap, or, hewn into planks, convey
The soul's frail vessel on the fragile top of the sea, the dead
Drift at large, or, stacked up
Nothing enters through the absent ports,—they cast
A backwards, inward gaze, a small amends, in that
What occurred appears in light
Of the conclusion, and at last they understand what really happened in
                              the dust and so they reach
As voices, out from corners, saying
What it is that one should mourn for, but their words
Are the thin whistles before sunrise, shrieks, spring's cats behind the
                              winter stone pile, a din
That rings the sleeper in his sleep.

It pierces me, that sleep
Which sleeplessness encounters, but the fear is not
That I may cease to be
But for all who go before me, left
A stranger to the populated earth. Then the ash,
Comfortless, claims me at the last, who would be only light
And deliberate fire.
Cheerless sleep, that, cradled by the human sea
And voices stream through dream's two horns like water birds,
Swans slowly drifting to the mouth of a dark sea.
Below, squid vanish in pools of ink.
If keeping back could keep that motion from me, I would never tread

The deathless beach, or gather sea chips cast up
By black winds, black salt winds like iron bearing down.

V

Only tales that return
Get told as the sun rises on the porches of the sun, where
Such shelter as the sky affords remains the aegis
Of divinity that men may apprehend both in and after storms:
The pools of peace are like the pools of anger in that water
Fills them at the last, and whatever visitation launched
Me hither now has borne me home again, the messenger
Whose charge has just begun to utter
Sentences that take a lifetime to complete.

Now each moment must appear the sum of all that went before:

the desert sinks
Beneath what has accumulated, a cloak
Of visibility wraps the hills that by attention rose in peaks before me.
What remains at rest could only be by-products
Of a vast activity for which the whole world stands,
Partly interpreted, evoked, in place
Of all that is intended.
Birds' wings transport them in their seasonal
migrations
Where no passage, even booked, could be assured.
Chance only makes a destiny
Look quirky, never makes what the sky has marked out
For its own: some birds fall
But eagles topple clangorous to the resounding earth
And if day's mirror then receives the pictures that we offer
It is because someone has gone before us, and prepared
The sky to listen.

Neither love
Nor fear can figure in the sky's selection, but a way of going
Still seems clear, now, by the risen sun
I greet what must be all my days advanced
Across the mural of impending

54

Speech, that carries me, the manifest
And form of sound and light, my father
Keep me to the last, and as the interval
That this edge occupies must lapse at times
Into my walking silence, so make recompense
For that lost sense by songs
Built with hard questions, lines that justify
And keep what letters always tend:
Those words by which whatever can ascends
Drawn by the force that stars are blown toward,
Drifting mass erected
By both wind and tide upon the water's edge.

THE POETRY READING: A MASQUE

performed at Cornell University, 2 November 1972

Enter the Spirit of History, wearing an ermine coat, carrying a whip, driving the Muse, a seventeen-year-old nymph in gauze with tissue wings, before him. The Muse turns and, opening her arms, induces History to dance with her. They dance. He drops his whip and spreads his coat on the ground. The couple lies down. Bells and violins. Six scholars in black gowns with long beards and tassels tow in a pyramid secured by a golden chain. The sides of the pyramid fall open, disclosing the Muse dressed in a white robe, wearing glasses, sitting by a table writing. A candle and a flashlight are on the table.

Enter General, leading hordes.

General.   By Pompey's pumps, the salt
      Crackers of Carthage, I've lost my taste
          My tactics faulty
      Continents and dynasties lie wasted
          But all to me seems
      Drear, dire, pale, soiled, soggy, blasted
          Not like dreams
      Of empire, triumphs and the virgins voting.

He sinks.

Muse.   The best
      Can't be had
          By the bad.
      What's guessed
          At not heard
      (Flesh made word)
          Flashes on the seas'
      Top, grows in peace.
          You vandals
      Are candles.

I stick
Your wick.

She snuffs the candle. The General disappears.

Muse.   Slanted afternoon, the speckled
                    Fractions days shackled
        To themselves can't be carried
                    Off by force. We varied
        Spouts and powers drone
                    On inside the pyramid we built
        That's not our own
                    That work we tilt.

*The moon rises. The Muse plucks the moon from overhead, and puts it
on the table next to the flashlight. A dog crosses the floor and exits. The
six scholars reappear, close up the sides of the pyramid, and drag it off.*

The Muse and History wake up on the ermine coat.

Muse.   O History, the lark
        Has spoke, the dark
        (No joke) has fled.
        Look. Lights prick
        Out, night's trick
        Has turned and you
        Stand warned. I'm blue.
        You're going

            (History departs)

        But I'll take heart,
        The poetry reading's about to start.

Here begins the anti-masque. The muse mounts the podium.

Muse.   The first Thursday in November,
        The month between October and December
        When light's short, and mud
        Not covered up with snow, but the blood

57

Of poets raging, thin with youth
Has brought them here in praise of truth
And beauty, sex, insanity's
Bathtubs, saloons, oak vanities
In boudoirs, stumps, they sing
   Of chilly spring
   And summer vile
And daybeds on mosaic tile.
They write from head and heart.
So let the reading start.

Muse steps down. Enter first poet, declaiming.

First Poet. O dire dirigibles, deflated
     Remember the Hindenburg and helium, inert
     As I, so young, am also gassed
     And with one spark might burst
     Like dictionaries' shoddy binding
     Which wouldn't be so bad but
     You have left me then, and O
     What can I do?

     I wrote this next poem under the influence
          Of aspirin: it's about pain
     And I would like to acknowledge the influence
          Of Master Charles, whose pain
     Was much like mine, but different, in that it had an influence
          On later sufferers from life, which I call pain.

PILL POEM

The bicycles lie flat
          upon the sidewalk
               their wheels
stopped
          turning.
               What
Huge force halted
          in the autumn air
               cerulean?

The wind
                    a knife
                                        cuts
what meets
                    it, boots
                                        or feather boa
constrictor, lurks
                    dissolving near
                                        the small intestine
the belly world.

This last poem is an experiment.
I hope you like the sentiment.

POEM

The birds have gone away.
The flowers have gone away.
Everything that lives has gone away.
Only I am here.

Exit first poet. Enter Poetess.

Poetess. I would like to read this poem about
        What I know best, myself
        And what I know is best
        About myself:

THE ALBATROSS

Who plants his thick green stem in my red pot?
The begonias have withered in the vase.
Do vases have vasectomies
Or does the flowery sap flow
Freely into the still water
And smell nice?
                My parents first came
In a garden, when the watchman
Caught them, and kicked them out.
O dread expulsion. Did they fall
Like seeds into the seedplot, sowing
What looks knowing, tamped, and puzzled?

59

I writhe on the point
I write with.
How could it happen that
Your daughter has grown
Into this, with sag marks
At Sagamore Hill?

That one was for Teddy, who kept me
Warm on winter nights when I was young, fearing harm.
But now I'm older, harm has come
To me, and harm has come to me.

*Three eager undergraduates assist her from the podium, strewing flowers
in her path. The Muse returns to the podium.*

Muse. In China poets often collaborated
 Writing link verse while drinking rice wine.
 Our next two poets have eaten Chinese dinner downtown and, sated,
 Returned to their modest rooms, feeling fine
 Put on their Li Po sweatshirts and composed
 The following short verses, here enclosed.
 Another note by way of introduction:
 Chinese poetry often provides a vehicle for practical instruction.

*The Muse steps down. The pair of Chinese poets mounts the podium.
One reads. The other stands silently by.*

Chinese poet:

BOTTLE ODE

The moon sat in the pasture.
The minister who drank with us returned to sit next to the wall
And I am desolate, like the Yellow River
That flows away from me and my companion
This dry bottle. Does sunlight
Penetrate the lotus?
The phoenix sighted in the west is smoke
And all my good advice has been rejected
By councilors in pointed hats who sit

Beside the wall, below the sun of heaven.

The tiger lillies and the tiger
Colored butterflies have joined the tiger
In the shadows. The river flows
Past the seated moon into the Yellow Sea
And I am desolate
Because my good advice has not been taken.

They step down. The Muse steps up.

Muse.   A real treat
     A local great
          Will now his verse
   Remonstrate.

*The Greek plasters lining the hall turn their heads at the arrival of the
Great Local, who floats in on a cloud of marijuana ringed with girls who
stroke his curls and fight to carry his verses. Falling like pears from a
pear tree in autumn, his entourage falls away, and the Great Local
mounts the podium.*

The Great Local.   Thank you. To understand this poem, you should refer to the
following: Blake's MILTON: A PROPHECY, Raymond Roussel's unpub-
lished diary of a winter at sea, the UPANISHADS, Gray's ANATOMY,
the last issue of PUBLISHERS WEEKLY, and my collected works which
may be had later at my apartment.

MARSUPIALIZATION

the pocket
in the pocket

the lining
lines lines

Orc sags
oak tag

This next poem was written while waiting for the E train at Christopher

61

Street. You must understand that I had just been attacked by a group of grammar-school-aged Puerto Rican children who forced me to perform an unspeakable act just after I had left a poetry reading where I had undergone a religious experience like the DIAMOND SUTRA and was going to visit my best friend's wife who used to hold my member when we were both kids in the slums of Dayton, Ohio, some thirty years ago.

THE INFINITE IMAGINATION IN A FINITE WORLD

the edge
of the poster
is torn and
ragged like
the torn
edge of
a poster

This last work is part of a projected long poem that shares its structure with the BOOK OF LAMENTATIONS and concerns the fall of a star from heaven, its discovery by a boy scout troop out on a rock hunt, and its subsequent exposure and destruction by the forces of publicity and the repressive and intolerable actions of certain small but priviledged elements that utilize police-state tactics to keep the works of the great twentieth-century poets (there are too many to name here) from coming to the attention of their puppet subjects who, if they heard these poems, would rise in arms against their oppressors and, if I may coin a phrase, build a New Jerusalem in this fair and pleasant land.

The star fell out of the sky.
The little children, scouts all
Picked it up and cried
"A star, a star"
But the scoutmaster took the star
Away from them, and placed it in
A big museum, circled it
With guards, and made
The children pay admission to watch
The star that was rightly theirs.
The star was sad.
Its light squibbed

62

Tender tears of light
And the keeper looked unhappy.
"Why don't you shine brighter,
Little star?"
But the star wouldn't answer.
It thought about the poets young
And mad and flaming on the telephone,
Of their later madness dying young, they arch
Like rainbows crashing in a river
Deep like time, but dirtied
By the foul pollutions of
Great men of power, who would not let
The star shine for free, or leave
The moon alone.

Thank you.

As the Great Local steps down from the podium, the donuts dance in rings around him, and the coffee cups make waffling noises, and spill their cream on the carpet. The Muse rises above the poetry reading, and hushes the hubbub with her spread wings.

Muse.   O let now all join up in a dance
To epic, allegory and romance,
To rhymes for blimp and frangipanes,
To terza and ottava rima,
Rime Royale, sestina,
Epigram, fourteener, Alexandrine, couplet, pantoum, sonnet,
            eclogue, villanelle, quantitative and blank verse,
Hexameter and madrigal, all flourishes that English can rehearse
Which must be to our greater glory
Who gathers here, the star in this short story.

So let's give thanks that we have tongues and ears
And manuscripts which must be souvenirs
Of this brief time we live in, which will pass
Like airplanes through our slipstreams, light through glass.

All rise and dance, and exit, dancing.

419 915